KU-504-639

PUFFIN BOOKS

UK | USA | Canada | Ireland | Australia
India | New Zealand | South Africa

Puffin Books is part of the Penguin Random House group of companies
whose addresses can be found at global.penguinrandomhouse.com.

www.penguin.co.uk
www.puffin.co.uk
www.ladybird.co.uk

First published 2019

001

Text copyright © Dr Sheila Kanani, 2019
Illustrations copyright © Nan Lawson, 2019

The moral right of the author and illustrator has been asserted

Text design by Janene Spencer
Printed and bound by CPI Group (UK) Ltd, Croydon, CR0 4YY

A CIP catalogue record for this book is available from the British Library

ISBN: 978–0–241–37279–1

All correspondence to:
Puffin Books, Penguin Random House Children's,
80 Strand, London WC2R 0RL

MIX
Paper from
responsible sources
FSC® C018179

Penguin Random House is committed to a
sustainable future for our business, our readers
and our planet. This book is made from Forest
Stewardship Council® certified paper.

ROSA
PARKS

Written by Dr Sheila Kanani
Illustrated by Nan Lawson

EXTRAORDINARY LIVES

PUFFIN

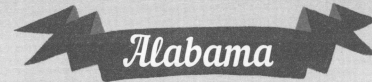

Alabama

Alabama
Where Rosa
was born

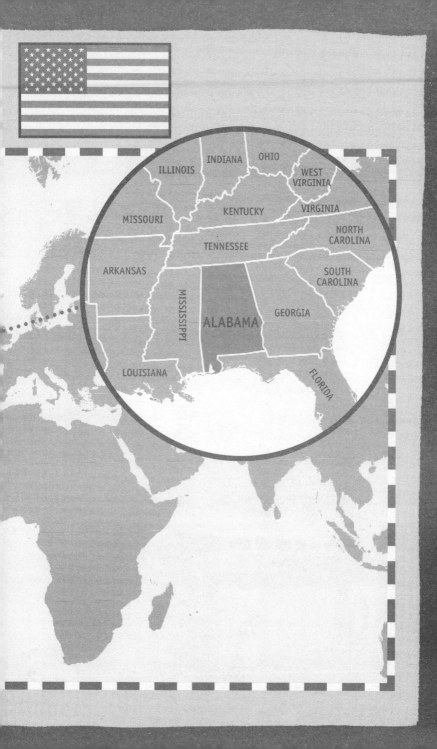

WHO WAS
Rosa Parks?

Rosa Parks

Rosa Louise McCauley was born on 4 February 1913
in Alabama in the United States of America.

By the time she was ninety-two years old she'd been awarded the *Presidential Medal of Freedom* and the *Congressional Gold Medal* by the American president Bill Clinton, and was known by many people as the *mother of the civil rights movement*. And it all started because of a bus.

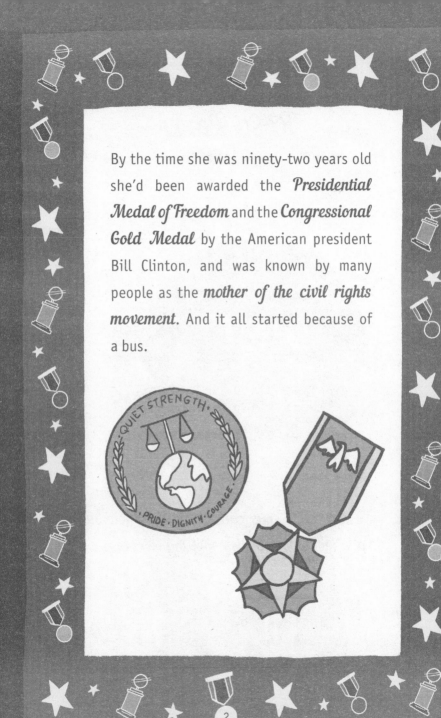

In those days there was racial segregation on public transport. This meant that black people were forced to sit in different areas from white people (usually towards the back of the bus).

Though Americans and the British both speak mainly English, the spelling of some of the words differs. Americans spell 'color' without a 'u', while the British spelling is 'colour'.

On 1 December 1955 Rosa had **just left work** for the day. She got on the bus, **paid her fare** and sat in the black section in an aisle seat.

If there were **no spaces left** in the white section of the bus, people in the black section could be asked to **stand up** so that white people were able to sit down.

As the journey went on, the bus started to **fill up**, so the driver asked four black people, **including Rosa**, to move. But **instead of getting up** to allow a white person to sit down, Rosa moved along just one seat to the **window**

seat to make space. She chose ***not to stand up***, and she was ***arrested*** for it.

Why didn't she give up her seat? She wasn't old, injured or tired from her work, but on that day she was ***tired of giving in***.

Rosa growing up

Rosa McCauley was born in 1913 in Tuskegee, Alabama, to parents Leona, who was a *teacher*, and James, who was a *carpenter*.

Rosa's ancestors were a mix of **African-American**, **Scots-Irish** and **Native American**, and Rosa was named after her **grandmother**.

Rosa's father had also been born in Alabama, in a place called Abbeville. He was light-skinned with wavy hair, and people often thought he was CHEROKEE.

In fact, James's grandmother (Rosa's **great-grandmother**) was a part Native American slave.

The CHEROKEE is the largest tribe of Native Americans in the USA.

James was really good at his job, and he built houses all over the Alabama *Black Belt region*, which was a large area with black clay soil. The soil was good for growing *cotton*, and many black people at that time were forced to work on cotton farms.

Leona, Rosa's mother, was a ***strict school teacher*** in Pine Level, Alabama, who believed in the value of ***education for everyone***. Leona trained to be a teacher through the African Methodist Episcopal Church (AME). She did not get a university degree because at the time it was forbidden for black women.

James and Leona were **_married_** on 12 April 1912 when they were both twenty-four years old. Rosa was born early the following year.

Not long after Rosa was born, her uncle (James's brother) came to live with the young family. Leona had had to leave her teaching job when she was pregnant, and it was a lonely time for her. But she was pleased that her daughter Rosa was born in *Tuskegee*, because it was said at the time that it was the **best place in Alabama** for African-Americans to educate themselves. When Rosa was very small her mother taught her the Alabama state MOTTO: *Audemus jura nostra defendere*, which means 'We dare defend our rights'.

This was an important message for Rosa to grow up believing in.

MOTTO:
a phrase that describes the intentions of an organization or people. Each of the fifty states in America has a motto.

Rosa grew up in a DILAPIDATED wooden house in Tuskegee, but **no one knows** exactly where the house is now, or even if it is still standing.

DILAPIDATED: run-down.

When she was young Rosa suffered from **_chronic tonsillitis_**, which made her very poorly quite often. Around this time she became heavily involved in the **_Christian church_**.

DID YOU KNOW?

At that time many white Christian people in America didn't want black people to be Christian, because they didn't like to think that black people had souls that deserved to go to heaven.

Rosa loved the HYMNS that her mother had sung to her as a baby.

HYMNS
are songs of praise to God.

'THE CHURCH, *with its musical rhythms* AND ECHOES OF AFRICA, ***thrilled me*** WHEN I WAS YOUNG.'

Until she was **nine years old**, Rosa was often BEDRIDDEN due to her tonsillitis.

It gave her a terribly **sore throat** and meant that swallowing was **really painful**. Because she had to stay in bed, Rosa didn't make many friends, and so the church became her **safe place**.

BEDRIDDEN: unable to leave bed.

The teachings of her **Christian religion** and important **black role models** such as Martin Lurther King Jr gave Rosa strength and courage, and always guided her to do the right thing. It was **difficult** growing up black in America when so many people were **racist**.

DID YOU KNOW?

Martin Luther King Jr was one of the most prominent and important leaders of the civil rights movement in America.

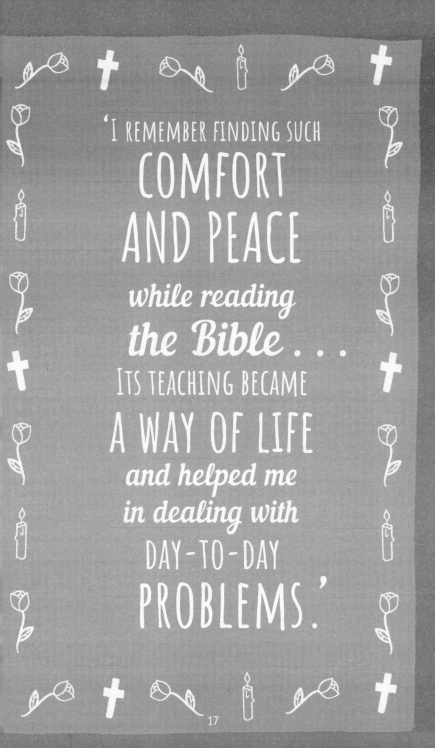

'I REMEMBER FINDING SUCH
COMFORT
AND PEACE
while reading
the Bible . . .
ITS TEACHING BECAME
A WAY OF LIFE
and helped me
in dealing with
DAY-TO-DAY
PROBLEMS.'

When Rosa was little there was an INFESTATION of weevils, a type of beetle, in Alabama, which destroyed the cotton plants, causing many crops to *fail* and a ***sudden collapse*** of many communities that relied on cotton.

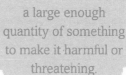

Infestation:
a large enough quantity of something to make it harmful or threatening.

This meant that Rosa's family had to move in with her grandparents and other family members, and the young family **shared a bedroom** that had a dirt floor. Leona didn't get on with James's parents and she found it **difficult** to bring up Rosa in these conditions. Eventually Leona decided to **move back to Pine Level** without James. Rosa barely saw her father again after that – only once when she was five years old and then again after she had grown up and married.

Back in Pine Level, Rosa, her mother and her younger brother, Sylvester, lived with Leona's parents. Leona was often teaching at black church schools, so Rosa and Sylvester were mostly looked after by their grandparents, who told the children about many great ACTIVISTS and black role models.

ACTIVIST: someone who strongly supports a cause and acts to make changes.

Growing up in the southern regions of the USA was difficult for a person of colour. African-American people had to abide by the discriminatory 'JIM CROW' LAWS.

THE JIM CROW LAWS

These were laws created by local governments that meant a lot of people had to live with racial segregation and discrimination because of the colour of their skin. The laws said that black people and white people had to have different schools, churches, offices, toilets and even drinking fountains.

'I knew there was SOMETHING WRONG with our way of life when people could be MISTREATED because of the color of their skin.'

The result was that African-American people *found it hard to vote*, had much *lower-paying jobs* and were *arrested for smaller crimes* than white people.

Early on, Rosa knew that she was *biracial*. Her brother Sylvester had very *fair skin*, and many people thought he was part Chinese. Her grandfather was also very pale, and was often *mistaken* as white.

Perhaps some of her grandfather's experiences gave Rosa the **spirit to stand up for herself** against racial discrimination.

DID YOU KNOW?

Even though interracial handshaking was forbidden, Rosa's grandfather would shake hands with white people, and they wouldn't suspect he was black because of his fair skin.

Growing up

As a young child Rosa was **quiet but curious**. Her family was known to **sing loudly in church**, and shout 'amen' and 'hallelujah' while she watched quietly. But their Christian enthusiasm still had a **profound effect** on little Rosa.

'God is EVERYTHING to me.'

Rosa remained *religious* throughout her life and was *proud of her church*, the AME. It had been *founded* by a former slave, and to this day the AME promotes *equality* for all Americans.

'It was the
SPIRITUAL
HOME
of many
WELL-KNOWN
BLACK PERSONS
in our history.'

By the time she turned nine years old, her mother had saved up enough money so that Rosa was able to have her tonsils removed in an *operation*, which made Rosa's life a lot better.

DID YOU KNOW?

Some people are given jelly and ice cream after they have their tonsils removed, to allow their throat to recover.

Even though Rosa had only lived in Tuskegee for a few years, she was greatly influenced by a man named BOOKER T. WASHINGTON.

Booker was an African-American activist, educator, adviser and former slave in the late nineteenth century, who gave rousing speeches and wrote useful texts for the black population of Tuskegee. His work influenced Rosa after his death in 1915.

When the family lived in Pine Level, Leona read extracts from Booker's books to Rosa, and the family *followed his teachings*. Some of these included keeping a clean home, working hard, saving money and making useful objects from everyday items, like baskets from pine needles and corn husks.

Rosa was also heavily influenced by her ***grandfather***. He had been a slave when he was a young boy, and as an adult he followed inspirational speakers who talked about making life better for black people. When Rosa was ten he wanted to attend a meeting held by one such speaker, but he was ***turned away*** at the door because they thought he was white! Rosa also remembered how he used to protect the family from the KU KLUX KLAN.

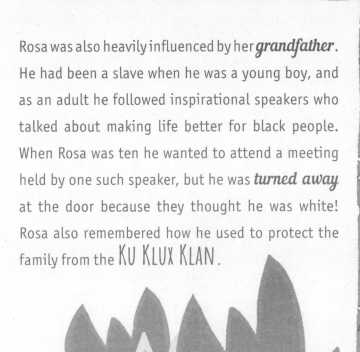

The KU KLUX KLAN were a group who hated black people, and would burn down black churches and hurt African-Americans.

Rosa's grandfather would sleep in the front room of the house while holding a gun, so that if the Ku Klux Klan were to try to hurt his family, he could **protect them**. He also made Rosa and Sylvester sleep fully clothed in case there was an attack in the middle of the night and the children had to **run away** as fast as they could. Rosa sometimes slept on the floor next to her grandfather.

Rosa also had to work in difficult conditions on the ***cotton farms***. As a child she was hired for ***fifty cents a day*** to pick cotton in the soaring heat. The black children who worked on the cotton farms didn't have shoes, and the sand burned their feet until they got blisters and bled. The children were ***forced*** to work from sunrise to sunset, and if they got blood on the white cotton, they could be whipped. When Rosa went to primary school she had to walk to get there, while the white children had special school buses available to them.

'To me, that was **A WAY OF LIFE;** we had no choice BUT TO ACCEPT WHAT WAS **THE CUSTOM.** The bus was among the first ways I realized THERE WAS A **BLACK WORLD** and a **WHITE WORLD.**'

Regardless of the **challenges** of being a young black girl during these times, Rosa had a **happy childhood**, playing hide-and-seek outdoors with her brother, singing in church, selling eggs and running through wildflower meadows.

Rosa enjoyed learning and went to local schools when she was young, then to the *Industrial School for Girls* in Montgomery, Alabama. It was a private school, and Rosa's family couldn't afford the tuition fees, so instead Rosa worked at the school, cleaning classrooms so that she could attend the classes. Her family knew it was her *best chance* at a good education.

At the school she learned practical skills like sewing, cooking and housekeeping – which were supposed to train her to be a good maid, housewife or mother in the future. It was a school for black girls, but all the teachers were white. The headmistress, Alice White, was a good example for Rosa of *self-worth and dignity*. Rosa was a *studious* child and completed all her lessons with pride.

The city of Montgomery was different from the small towns where Rosa had grown up. She became more aware of the struggles of black people, and learned more about **segregation**. During one of her lessons she heard about black ministers in 1900 who asked people to BOYCOTT the local transport at the time, streetcars (trams).

BOYCOTT:
a voluntary and intentional refusal to do or buy a certain thing.

WE STAND AGAINST SEGREGATION

FIGH for your RIGHTS

They asked everyone to **walk** instead, and this worked because the streetcars started to lose money. For a while black people were allowed to sit **wherever they wanted** on the streetcars. Hearing about this boycott must have really stuck in Rosa's mind.

The Industrial School closed in 1928 when Alice White became ill and left Montgomery. *No one else* wanted to take over because many white people held the BIGOTED view that black girls should not be educated.

JIM CROW MUST GO!

BIGOTED:
Prejudiced

When the school closed, Rosa went to a different secondary school that was set up by the Alabama State Teachers College for NEGROES.

NEGRO is an old term for a black person, particularly those from south of the Sahara desert in Africa, and it is considered an offensive term.

However, Rosa had to leave formal education when she was sixteen because she had to care for her **elderly** grandparents and, eventually, her sick mother. Rosa had **dreamed of being a teacher**, like her mother, but because of leaving her education early she instead had various other jobs, such as working in a **textile factory** and as a **housekeeper**.

When Rosa was eighteen she was working as a *housekeeper*, and her spare time was dedicated to her church, the AME in Montgomery. Through a mutual friend she met a man called *Raymond Parks*, who was a barber and a caretaker at her church.

Raymond had the same *values* as Rosa, and had also spent a lot of time caring for sick relatives, just like she had. He immediately fell for Rosa, but she *turned him down* a few times before eventually agreeing to go on a date with him!

Their **_first date_** took place in Raymond's **_shiny red car_**. Rosa liked that Raymond was similar to her, as he also felt very **_strongly_** about the rights of black Americans and he was a well-educated man who read a lot of books.

When Rosa first met Raymond he was very involved in a criminal case protecting the **SCOTTSBORO BOYS**.

DID YOU KNOW?

THE SCOTTSBORO BOYS were a group of nine black teenagers and young men. They were train-hopping, looking for work, when a fight broke out between them and seven white boys. The white boys started the fight, and the black boys managed to throw the white boys off the train at Scottsboro. The white boys reported what had happened to the local sheriff, who arrested the black boys. By the time the black boys were put in jail they had been falsely accused of attacking two white female passengers. The case went to court and the boys were found guilty by a white jury, even though there was no evidence at all.

Raymond and his friends and colleagues in the **NAACP** raised money for the boys so that they could have another trial with a proper lawyer.

NAACP:
National Association for the Advancement of Colored People, an organization formed in response to violence against black people in America.

Rosa really *admired* Raymond for his work on the Scottsboro Boys case, and when he proposed to her in 1931 she accepted. They were married in 1932.

The Scottsboro Boys were all retried and eventually **cleared of all the charges**, although the last of the boys was only freed in 1950, nineteen years after he was first arrested. This criminal case, and her involvement through Raymond, lit a fire inside Rosa.

In 1933 Raymond urged Rosa to *go back and complete high school*.

When Rosa finished school, only 7 per cent of African Americans actually had the opportunity to do so.

Over the next few years Rosa had a few different jobs, including being a *seamstress* and *nurse's assistant*. In 1941 she got a job as a secretary at Maxwell Air Force Base, which was *unsegregated*. This was a whole new experience for Rosa.

Rosa was *amazed* to see white people and black people being treated equally. She felt free. She could sit *anywhere she wanted* on the air base's buses.

But as soon as she went home her life went back to how it had always been, *separated* from white people.

It became worse when the soldiers returned home, as black VETERANS were often treated badly.

VETERAN: someone who has previously served in the army.

Sylvester had thought that his service to his country would mean he would get more *respect* from white Americans, but instead black veterans were often abused physically and verbally. It seemed especially awful that the freedoms they had fought for were not extended to them when they returned.

Eventually Sylvester and his young family moved away to *Detroit, Michigan*, and Rosa missed them terribly.

Rosa's boycotts

*F*rom 1900 there were **specific rules** about black people using buses in Montgomery. Bus conductors had the power to split people up on the buses depending on the colour of their skin. It wasn't the law that black people had to give up their seats to white people, but, over time, the bus conductors made it **common practice**.

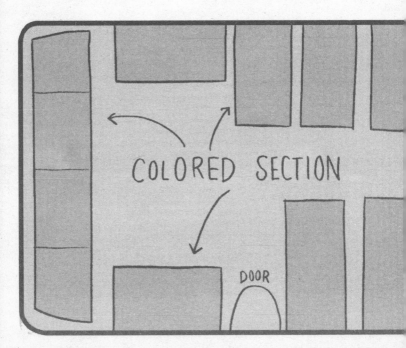

COLORED SECTION

DOOR

By law the first four rows of seats were for white people, and black people had to sit at the back. Often the areas for black people were **small**, even though generally there were **more black people** riding the buses than white people. The sections were not fixed, and the bus conductor could **move a sign** to change where the black section began. If the bus wasn't busy, black people could sit in the middle sections, but if there were more white people on the bus, black people had to move to the back, or **get off**.

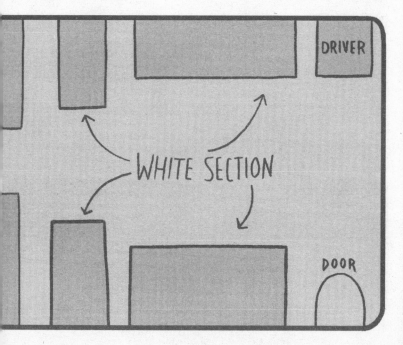

Black people could not sit in the **_same row_** as white people, or even **_across the aisle_** from them. The driver could even **_remove the sign completely_** so no black people could ride the bus, if he wanted. And if there were white people sitting at the front of the bus when a black person got on, the black person had to get off the bus, and return via the back door.

In 1943 Rosa had her first **run-in** with a bus driver called James Blake. It was a cold November day and Rosa got on the bus, paid her fare to the driver at the front, then went to continue down **through the bus** into the black area. But the rules at the time meant she had to **get off the bus** and re-enter through the back door.

WHITE

Rosa stood her ground because she knew that this was *unfair*. The bus driver pulled at her coat, insisting that she stuck to the rules. She got off the bus, and the driver pulled away, leaving Rosa *stranded*, even though she had paid for her journey.

Fighting for rights

In December 1943 Rosa joined the NAACP herself, becoming more active in CIVIL RIGHTS issues.

CIVIL RIGHTS:
the rights and freedoms that each person has.

As she was the *only woman* in that part of the NAACP, she became the *secretary* (because it was the sort of job expected to be done by women at the time) for its director, E. D. Nixon.

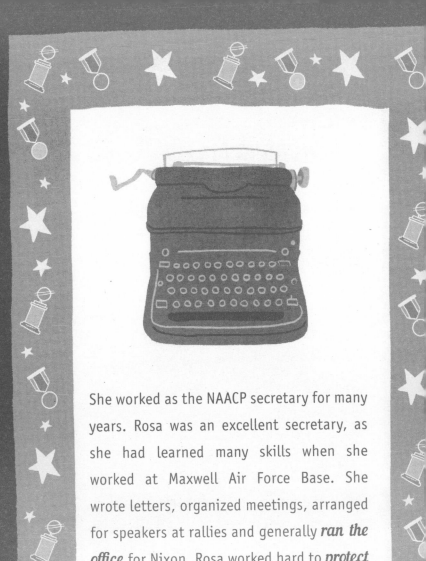

She worked as the NAACP secretary for many years. Rosa was an excellent secretary, as she had learned many skills when she worked at Maxwell Air Force Base. She wrote letters, organized meetings, arranged for speakers at rallies and generally **ran the office** for Nixon. Rosa worked hard to **protect other people**, and did a lot for the rights of African-Americans.

She also **volunteered** with young black children, taking them on field trips and teaching them about **important issues** like racism. In time, she became great friends with a woman named Virginia Durr.

Virginia Durr was from a **wealthy white family**, but when she had been at college she had seen the awful effects of segregation and had **vowed to help** African-American people. Rosa sewed clothes for the Durr children and Virginia said that Rosa was one of the **greatest people** she had ever met.

In August 1955 Rosa Parks met *Martin Luther King Jr.* She would meet him again just a few months later.

On 1 December 1955 Rosa was on her way home from her work as a seamstress in a department store, which involved **taking the bus**. She got on the bus, paid her fare and went to sit in the black section. On this particular day the section started around the middle of the bus, and she sat in **the first row of the black section**. She didn't realize at the time that the driver was **James Blake**, the same man who had forced her off his bus in 1943.

'All I was doing was TRYING TO GET HOME FROM WORK.'

As the bus continued on its
way many **more white people** got on, so
the driver decided to change where the black
section of the bus started. He **moved the sign behind
Rosa**, and asked her and some other people to move
to allow the white passengers to sit down.

'When that
WHITE DRIVER
stepped back toward us,
WHEN HE WAVED HIS HAND
AND ORDERED US UP
AND OUT OF OUR SEATS,
I felt a
DETERMINATION
cover my body
LIKE A QUILT
on a winter night.'

The three other people did as they were told, including the man sitting next to Rosa. When he moved to the back of the bus Rosa *moved into his seat*. But this wasn't what James Blake had asked.

James Blake shouted at Rosa to move, and she said that she didn't think she should have to. He said that if she didn't, he would *call the police* and have her arrested. Rosa calmly said that he could do just that.

As the scene unfolded Rosa found herself thinking about a young boy who had been murdered earlier that year because of the colour of his skin.

'People always said that
I DIDN'T GIVE UP MY SEAT
BECAUSE I WAS TIRED,
but that isn't true.
I WAS NOT TIRED PHYSICALLY,
*or no more tired than
I usually was at the end
of a working day.*
I WAS NOT OLD,
*although some people have an
image of me as being old then . . .*
No, THE ONLY TIRED I WAS,
WAS TIRED OF GIVING IN.'

Change is coming

Rosa was arrested by a police officer, and felt *humiliated and angry* that this could happen. She was fined for breaking the law, but *refused* to pay the money because she did not agree with the laws of segregation, and she felt strongly that she was *not guilty*.

Over the next few days many people in the black community *discussed* what to do. People like E. D. Nixon, Rosa's boss at the NAACP, Jo Ann Robinson, a member of the Women's Political Council, and Martin Luther King Jr, the leader of the newly formed Montgomery Improvement Association, had *spread the word* that there was going to be a *bus boycott*. This meant that from 5 December 1955 African-American people in Montgomery *refused to use public transport*, instead walking to where they needed to go.

On the morning of 5 December it was also Rosa's ***court trial***. She had 500 supporters in court ***rooting for her***. Her court hearing lasted half an hour and she was fined $14 for her 'crime'.

But by this time her quiet act had **spurred** something much bigger into action. As the boycott began, bus companies started to lose money because most of the people who used the buses were black. Many African-American people found the boycott difficult, as they did not have cars and had to **walk huge distances** to continue their normal lives, but they stuck together to **make their voices heard.**

The boycott wasn't just about being forced to give up seats on buses. The boycotters promised to stop using the buses until black people were treated with courtesy, until black drivers were hired, and until seating in the middle of the bus was on a first-come basis.

'AT THE TIME I WAS **ARRESTED** I had no idea it would TURN INTO THIS. It was just a day like any other day. THE ONLY THING THAT MADE IT **SIGNIFICANT** was that the masses of the people joined in.'

About **_forty thousand_** black commuters chose to walk to work, some having to walk up to twenty miles.

A healthy person can walk about three miles per hour, so twenty miles would have taken, on average, about seven hours!

The boycott was a **_huge success_** and lasted 381 days – more than a **_whole year_**! By the end of the boycott in 1956 it was decided that the Jim Crow laws were UNCONSTITUTIONAL.

UNCONSTITUTIONAL: at odds with America's political system.

With such an excellent victory Rosa Parks became known as 'the mother of the civil rights movement' and the **_Montgomery Bus Boycott_** went down in history as one of the largest and most successful group **_movements against racial segregation_** that the world had ever seen.

After the boycott

*B*ut even though the laws had changed, things ***did not*** get much easier. Black political leaders were attacked and their houses were bombed, and many threats were made to Rosa and Raymond.

Rosa *lost her job* at the department store and Raymond was fired because he was *forbidden* to talk about his wife or her court case. In 1957 the Parks decided to move to *Detroit*, where Rosa's brother, Sylvester, and his family were living.

Rosa had high hopes for the move because Detroit was supposed to be a very PROGRESSIVE city.

PROGRESSIVE:
looking forward and making positive changes.

But when she arrived, Rosa found it hard to see any improvement, as forms of *segregation and racism* were still widespread. Rosa CAMPAIGNED against housing segregation, and continued to help those less fortunate than herself.

CAMPAIGN:
to fight in support of a particular cause.

'You must
NEVER BE FEARFUL
about what you
are doing
WHEN IT IS RIGHT.'

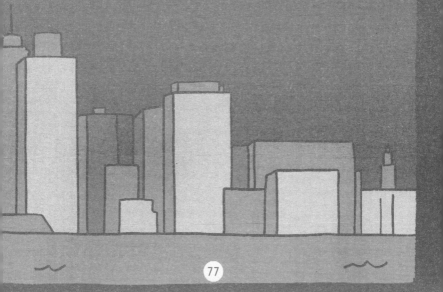

Rosa took on various jobs, including, in 1964, becoming a **deaconess** in the AME, which she was so fond of. She started working for a man called John Conyers in 1965, who was running for a place in Congress (the collection of people who have the power to **change the law** in the American government). She became his secretary when he was elected to Congress, and she introduced him to Martin Luther King Jr.

This was a **bold move**, but it turned out to be a really good one for both John Conyers and Martin Luther King Jr.

Rosa's daily work for Conyers included being his receptionist and secretary, but she was also able to focus on *important issues*, like welfare, education, affordable housing and jobs for African-Americans. She visited schools and hospitals, and *always spoke up* and told Conyers what was important for the black community and civil rights.

'You treated her with

DEFERENCE

because she was so quiet, so serene – just a very

SPECIAL PERSON . . .

There was

ONLY ONE ROSA PARKS.'

– John Conyers

Rosa was very active in **campaigning** for many things. She attended marches, gave rousing speeches and supported her comrades.

DID YOU KNOW?

Rosa was right by Martin Luther King Jr's side when he gave his famous 'I Have a Dream' speech in 1963. Have you listened to that speech?

She also became friends with Malcolm X, another black human rights activist, who she regarded as a *huge influence*.

Rosa was strongly affected by the discrimination that black people experienced when it came to **housing**. She lived in the Virginia Park district of Detroit, where lots of buildings were torn down and black people **lost their homes.** There were riots and fights in this district because of the inequality there. Rosa took part in many movements and conferences to make Virginia Park a better place.

She helped open the first black shopping centre there, and assisted the local council in **rebuilding** the area.

Continuing to fight

As the years went on Rosa fought *tirelessly* for the rights of black Americans. She organized for some *political prisoners* to be released, and she supported Joan Little and Gary Tyler, who were wrongly accused of crimes because of the colour of their skin.

FREE JOAN LITTLE

FREE GARY TYLER

'I believe there is

ONLY

ONE

RACE

- the human race.'

But during this time Rosa's personal life took many knocks. Both Rosa and her husband spent time in hospital due to illness, and Rosa spent most of her money on hospital bills. She gave much of the rest of her money to **charity**, so she was not a wealthy woman, even though by now she was *quite famous*.

Her husband, Raymond, and her brother, Sylvester, both died from cancer in 1977. Rosa started to step away from campaigning and activism. Perhaps this was how she coped with loss and grief.

A few years later, Rosa suffered a fall and had some bad *injuries*, so she moved into a nursing home with her mother, Leona. There she looked after her mother until Leona passed away in 1979 at the age of ninety-two.

In 1980 she set up the **Rosa L. Parks Scholarship Foundation** to support high-school students who couldn't afford college fees, and she used a lot of her own money (which she got from giving public speeches).

In 1987 Rosa and a friend, Elaine Eason Steele, opened the *Rosa and Raymond Parks Institute for Self Development* in honour of Raymond. The institute was for young black Americans, to educate and motivate them. By this time Rosa was in her seventies, and she was getting more frail, but she still managed to campaign and give speeches to eager audiences.

The Rosa and Raymond Parks Institute for
Self Development worked mostly with young
people under eighteen, who were able to
meet Rosa and other important figures, and
learn about and help with historical and
educational **research** all over the world.
Rosa wanted them to **learn about who they
were**, where their families had come from,
and to think about where they might end up
in life. Rosa, quiet but courageous, became
a **role model** for young people everywhere.
But she was always modest and encouraged
young people to learn about other
significant figures too.

In 1992 Rosa wrote an **AUTOBIOGRAPHY** and continued to make public appearances.

AUTOBIOGRAPHY: a book that someone writes about their own life.

'Each person
must
LIVE THEIR LIFE
AS A MODEL
for others.'

In 1994 Rosa was robbed and attacked in her own home by a man named Joseph Skipper. He was sent to prison. After this Rosa was too afraid to return to her home, and she moved into an apartment complex. Various people donated money to help her during her later years, including the founder of a pizza chain who had admired what she had done for the city of Detroit.

DID YOU KNOW?

In 1994 the racist organization the Ku Klux Klan gave money to the Missouri council to sponsor a motorway in America. The council accepted the money, but named that portion of the motorway after Rosa, calling it the Rosa Parks Highway!

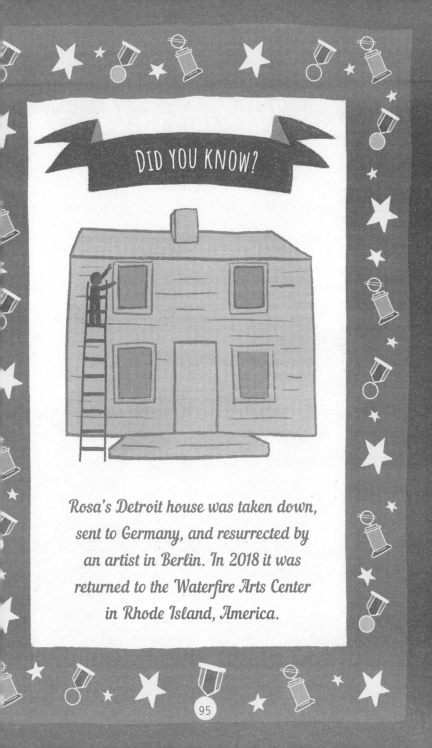

Rosa's Detroit house was taken down, sent to Germany, and resurrected by an artist in Berlin. In 2018 it was returned to the Waterfire Arts Center in Rhode Island, America.

Her last days

Vntil Rosa died she was **well looked after** by family, friends, her church and the people of Detroit. She was loved, honoured and admired, because all her life she had supported other people, often **putting others before herself**.

'RACISM

is still with us.

BUT IT IS UP TO US

to prepare

our children

FOR WHAT THEY

HAVE TO MEET,

and, hopefully,

WE SHALL

OVERCOME.'

Rosa died peacefully in her apartment on 24 October 2005. On 27 October 2005 every bus in Montgomery and Detroit had **black ribbons tied to the front seats** to honour Rosa Parks. Her coffin was taken to her AME church in Montgomery for the public to visit.

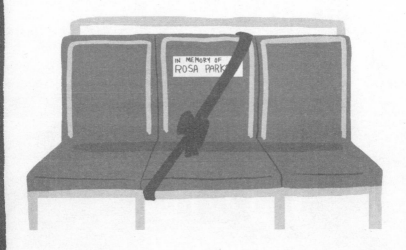

One of the speakers at the church service was Condoleezza Rice, the US SECRETARY OF STATE at the time. Condoleezza was the first female African-American secretary of state.

The SECRETARY OF STATE is a very high-power position in the American government.

'I CAN HONESTLY SAY
that without *Mrs Parks*,
I PROBABLY WOULD
NOT BE STANDING HERE

TODAY

as secretary of state.'

– Condoleezza Rice

After the service in Montgomery, Rosa's coffin was taken to the rotunda at the US Capitol, Washington DC, to lie in state. The coffin was transported by a bus similar to the one that she had made her protest in. She was the *first woman* and only the *second black person* to be honoured in this way. A memorial service while her coffin was at the US Capitol was broadcast on national television, and over 50,000 people visited. Her coffin then went to

Detroit for the public to view, and to the Greater Grace Temple Church for her funeral, which lasted *seven hours*.

After her funeral an honour guard **laid the US flag** over her coffin, which was taken by horse-drawn hearse to Woodlawn Cemetery in Detroit. Thousands of people lined the streets to watch the procession, clapping, cheering and releasing white balloons.

Rosa's body was finally laid to rest between her husband, Raymond, and her mother, Leona, at the Woodlawn Cemetery in the chapel mausoleum. This chapel was later renamed the *Rosa L. Parks Freedom Chapel*. Rosa had **prepared her own headstone** before she died, to sit along side those of her mother and husband.

Her legacy

Rosa led a full life and her legacy continued well after her death. She earned forty-two ***honorary degrees*** from universities across the globe, wrote books and had books written about her, starred in TV programmes and films, and had songs written about her. She was awarded the Presidential Medal of Freedom by President Bill Clinton in 1996 and the Congressional Gold Medal in 1999, and had a ***day named in her honour*** – Rosa Parks Day.

She has various buildings, museums, roads, sports arenas, bus stops and libraries named after her; she was voted by *Time* magazine to be in the top twenty most influential people of the twentieth century; she met **Nelson Mandela** in 1990 and **Pope John-Paul II** in 1999; and she was awarded more medals, prizes and certificates than many people alive today! She has been honoured in popular culture, in film, television and in most music genres from grime to hip hop, and she has a statue in National Statuary Hall, Washington DC. She also has an asteroid named after her: 284996 Rosaparks.

'IN A SINGLE MOMENT, *with the* SIMPLEST OF GESTURES, *she helped change America –* AND CHANGE THE WORLD.'

– President Barack Obama, on the unveiling of the Rosa Parks statue.

Not bad for a quiet, modest, dignified but infinitely courageous woman.

'I would like to be known as A PERSON WHO IS CONCERNED ABOUT

FREEDOM
and
EQUALITY
and
JUSTICE
and
PROSPERITY
for all people.'

TIMELINE

4 February 1913

Rosa Louise McCauley born
in Tuskegee, Alabama, USA.

1931

Rosa becomes more
interested in politics after
learning about the case of
the Scottsboro Boys.

18 December 1932

Rosa marries
Raymond Parks.

December 1943

Becomes secretary of the Montgomery NAACP.

1941

Starts working at Maxwell Air Force Base, which was unsegregated.

1943

Rosa is forced off a bus for not re-entering at the back.

3 June 1946

The US Supreme Court bans segregation in bus travel across American states. However, the southern states refuse to obey this ruling.

August 1955

Rosa meets Martin Luther King Jr.

1 December 1955

Rosa is arrested for not giving up her seat for a white man. Montgomery Bus Boycott starts on 5 December.

20 December 1956

Segregation law ruled to
be 'unconstitutional'.
Montgomery Bus
Boycott ends.

COLORED

WHITES

1957

Rosa moves to Virginia,
then to Detroit,
Michigan.

28 August 1963

Martin Luther King Jr makes
his famous 'I Have a Dream'
speech.

1965

Rosa Parks hired as a
secretary to John Conyers.

1979

Rosa Parks is
awarded the
Spingarn Medal
by the NAACP.

FOR
MERIT

1980

Receives the Martin
Luther King Jr Award
from the NAACP.

1987

Rosa co-founds the Rosa
and Raymond Parks
Institute for Self
Development.

30 August 1994

Rosa, aged eighty-one,
is attacked at home.

9 September 1996

Rosa is awarded the Presidential
Medal of Freedom by President
Bill Clinton.

1998

Receives the International Freedom Conductor Award by the National Underground Railroad Freedom Center.

1999

Awarded the Congressional Gold Medal.

Named by *Time* magazine as one of the twenty most influential figures of the century.

24 October 2005

Rosa Parks dies, aged ninety-two.

30 October 2005

Rosa's body lies in state in the US Capitol rotunda, the first woman to be given the honour.

2013

Statue of Rosa Parks placed in National Statuary Hall in Washington DC.

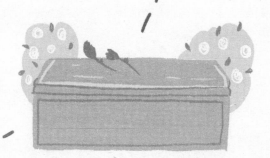

'WE WOMEN ARE FORTUNATE
to scan the generations and
discover women who dared to be

"SHEROES"
and role models for girls
and young women.
MADAME CURIE,
HARRIET TUBMAN,
ELEANOR ROOSEVELT,
AND MRS ROSA PARKS
have brightened our days and influenced
our thoughts. Because of their courage

and insight, we have come to believe we can be the best and deserve the best.

THANKS TO ALL OF THEM.'

– Maya Angelou

Can you think of some people - of any gender - who have been amazing role models to you? What have they done that has inspired you?

Index

Quote Sources

Quotes throughout are from *Rosa Parks: A Life* (Douglas Brinkley, Penguin Books, November 2005) except the below:

Page 22: *The Rebellious Life of Mrs. Rosa Parks* (Jeanne Theoharris, Beacon Press, December 2015)

Page 34: 'Rosa Parks "Transformed a Nation" on this day in 1955' (Sha Be Allah, www.thesource.com/2014/12/01/rosa-parks-transformed-a-nation-on-this-day-in-1955/)

Page 61: 'Rosa Parks' (*Time* Magazine, 15 December 1975)

Page 63: *The Thunder of Angels: The Montgomery Bus Boycott and the People who Broke the Back of Jim Crow* (Donnie Williams and Wayne Greenhaw, Chicago Review Press, 2005)

Page 66: *Rosa Parks: My Story* (Rosa Parks and James Haskin, Puffin, 1992)

Page: 71: 'Rosa Parks, Civil Rights Pioneer, Dies' (NY Times, www.nytimes.com/2005/10/25/world/americas/rosa-parks-civil-rights-pioneer-dies.html, October 2005,)

Page 77: 'Rosa Parks and Civil Disobedience' (Prerana Korpe, www.newseum.org/2015/12/01/rosa-parks-and-civil-disobedience/, December 2015)

Page 80: 'Parks Remembered for her Courage, Humility' (CNN, www.edition.cnn.com/2005/US/10/25/parks.reax/index.html, October 2005,)

Page 85: AZ Quotes (www.azquotes.com/quote/1146287)

Page 93: AZ Quotes (www.azquotes.com/quote/225373)

Page 97: Library of Congress: www.loc.gov/item/2018647571/)

Page 99: Condoleezza Rice memorial speech for Rosa Parks, October 2005

Page 107: National Women's Hall of Fame (www.womenofthehall.org/inductee/rosa-parks/)

Pages 116–117: 'Rosa Parks Honored in Quotes' (www.biography.com/news/rosa-parks-honored-in-quotes-21116113)

Have you read about all of these extraordinary people?

THE EXTRAORDINARY LIFE OF
STEPHEN HAWKING

THE EXTRAORDINARY LIFE OF
MICHELLE OBAMA

THE EXTRAORDINARY LIFE OF
MALALA YOUSAFZAI

THE EXTRAORDINARY LIFE OF
ANNE FRANK

THE EXTRAORDINARY LIFE OF
KATHERINE JOHNSON

THE EXTRAORDINARY LIFE OF
NEIL ARMSTRONG

THE EXTRAORDINARY LIFE OF
MARY SEACOLE

THE EXTRAORDINARY LIFE OF
ROSA PARKS

THE EXTRAORDINARY LIFE OF
MAHATMA GANDHI